LOOK AT
COLOUR AND
CAMOUFLAGE

Franklin Watts
96 Leonard Street
London EC2 4RH

Franklin Watts Inc.
387 Park Avenue South
New York
N.Y. 10016

Franklin Watts Australia
14 Mars Road
Lane Cove
N.S.W. 2066

UK ISBN: 0 86313 982 5

Editor: Ruth Thomson

Design: K and Co.
Consultant: Julian Hector
Illustrations: Simon Roulstone
Typeset by Lineage, Watford
Printed in Italy
by G. Canale & C.S.p.A., Turin

Picture credits:
Heather Angel 18, 19, 26b, 26c, 27a, 27b, 27c, 28a, 28b, 29c
Bruce Coleman 10, 14, 22, 23
Chris Fairclough 9
Oxford Scientific Films 16b, 17, 24, 25
Neil Thomson 5c
Science Photo Library 5a
Survival Anglia 20, 28c, 29b
Peter Newark's Military Pictures 4b
Zefa 4a, 5b, 6a, 6b, 7a, 7b, 8, 11, 12, 13, 15, 16a, 21, 26a, 29a

LOOK AT
COLOUR AND
CAMOUFLAGE

Rachel Wright

FRANKLIN WATTS

London • New York • Sydney • Toronto

We wear coloured clothes
for different reasons.

Soldiers wear colours that match
their surroundings.
This makes it harder
for their enemies to spot them.

In the past, soldiers wore bright
red uniforms to scare their enemies,
and to be seen.

We recognise doctors
by their white coats.

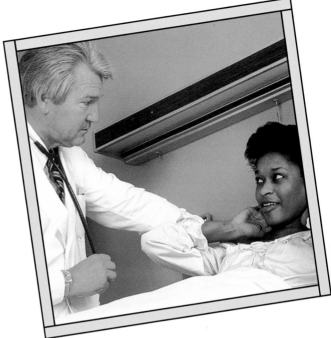

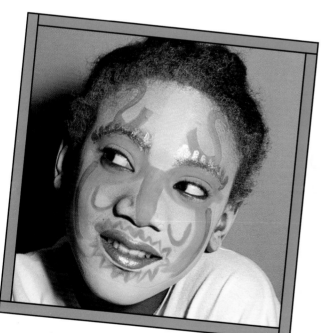

We dress up and colour our faces
to get ourselves noticed.

Animals use their colours and patterns
in a similar way.
Do you know why some animals are patterned
and others are not.
Or why some are brightly coloured
and others are not?

Field mouse

Butterfly fish

Kingfisher

Leopard

Many birds and insects see in colour.
They can see a bigger range of colours than humans.
Their colouring helps them to recognise or signal to each other.

Parrots

Most mammals, such as dogs and cats, don't see in colour.
They see only pale colours or shades of grey.
Colour is not important to them.
This is why so many are dully coloured.

Labrador

Some animals have bright colours
to attract a mate.
Male birds of paradise dance and show off
their coloured feathers to the females.

Coral fish use their bright colours as signals to recognise each other.

Poisonous insects and those with a sting
are often black and yellow.
These colours warn their enemies
not to attack them.

Bumble bee

Hover fly

Some harmless insects are
black and yellow too.
They are called mimics.
Their colours fool their enemies
into thinking they are dangerous.

The peacock butterfly also uses colour
to protect itself.
With its wings folded, it looks helpless.

If it is disturbed,
it will suddenly open its wings
to reveal two big, coloured eyespots.
These frighten away its enemy.

Tiger

Texas horned lizard

Many animals have colours that match
their surroundings.
These make it difficult for them to be seen.
This is called camouflage.

Insect-eating bats search for food at night.
Their dark colouring makes it hard for their prey to spot them against the night sky.

Nightjar

Hunted animals also use camouflage.
Female birds are often drab,
so that they will be camouflaged
when sitting on their nests.

Flatfish live mainly on the seabed.
Their markings look like specks of sand,
so their outline is hard to see.

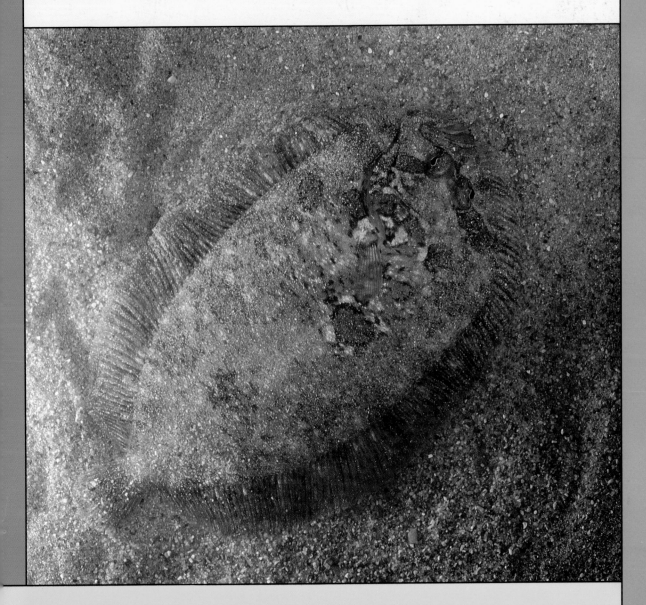

Zebras graze and move about in herds.
From a distance their stripes appear to blend.
This protects the herd from attack.

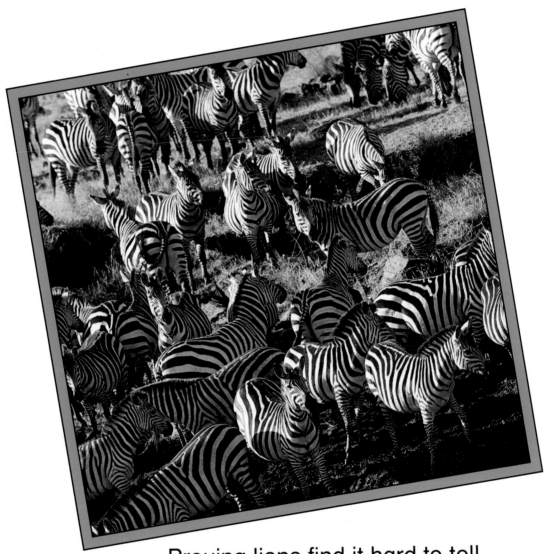

Preying lions find it hard to tell
one zebra from another.

Arctic animals have light-coloured coats.
This is useful camouflage in the snow,
for both hunters and the hunted.
This Arctic fox is a hunter.

Some creatures change their colour
as they grow older.
Baby tapirs are patterned, which helps
to camouflage them in the undergrowth.
Adult tapirs have dark coats,
so they won't be seen when they feed at night.

Some male freshwater fish are brightly coloured
when they are very angry or excited.
Their colour fades as they calm down.

Some animals that live in the Arctic all the time,
change colour in summer and winter.
This way they are camouflaged
all year round.

The white-tailed ptarmigan is white
in winter...

and changes to brown as summer approaches.

Chameleons can change their colour
to match their surroundings...

so can bell-frogs.

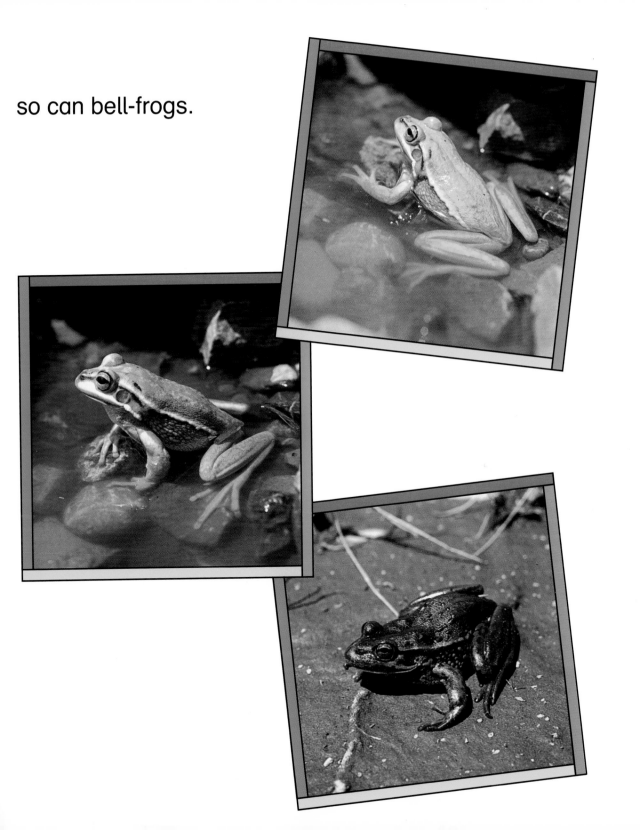

In each picture, there is
a well-camouflaged animal.
Can you see
where they are hiding?

Viper

Lynx

Leaf fish

Oak beauty moth

Ptarmigan

Crayfish

Do you know?

● The colour of birds' eggs often helps to camouflage them.

Nightjars, terns and plovers lay their eggs out in the open, not in a nest. The colour of the eggs matches the ground on which they are laid.

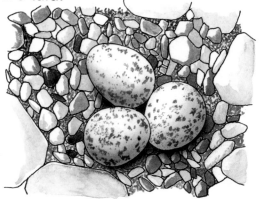

The wood pigeon's eggs are white. Their flimsy nests have see-through bottoms. If you stood underneath the nest and looked up, the eggs look like the sky and are difficult to see.

Owls' eggs are glossy white, so that their parents can see them in the dark.

● Some animals change colour as the moisture in the air changes. Toads become paler in dry, warm weather. Pale colour reflect more heat and this helps to keep it cool.

● Decorator crabs have tiny, curved bristles on their shells. Bits of seaweed and other materials hook on to their bristles. This helps to camouflage them.

● As far as anyone knows, octopuses cannot see in colour. This is strange, since they are able to turn from white to red in seconds.

● Many fish are brightly coloured. In general, the more brightly coloured a fish, the more aggressive it is.

Things to do

● Keep a camouflage scrapbook. Collect pictures of animals camouflaged against different backgrounds. Make separate sections for those which change colour with the seasons, those that change colour with age and those that change colour with mood.

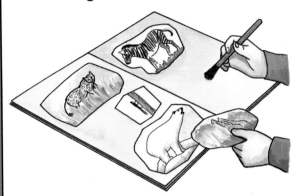

● Draw or model some scenery. Add an animal or bird whose colours blend in with those you have already used.

● When you next visit the zoo, make a note of all the brightly coloured animals and birds that you see. Try to find out why they are so brightly coloured.

Words and sayings

Can you find out what these words and sayings mean?

colour blind
false colours
off colour
colourful
colourless
colour line
colour up
high colour
primary colours

To lose colour
To come out in one's true colours
To come off with flying colours
To nail one's colours to the mast
To eat one's colours
Fear no colours
Under colour of

Index